SPRINKLER

SNAIL

CLOUD

FIREFLY

My thanks to Mrs. Twyman

—L.C.E.

COPYRIGHT © 2011 BY LISA CAMPBELL ERNST

ALL RIGHTS RESERVED / CIP DATA IS AVAILABLE.

PUBLISHED IN THE UNITED STATES 2011 BY

🍎 BLUE APPLE BOOKS

515 VALLEY STREET, MAPLEWOOD, NJ 07040

WWW.BLUEAPPLEBOOKS.COM

FIRST EDITION   03/11

PRINTED IN DONGGUAN, CHINA

ISBN: 978-1-60905-009-2

1 3 5 7 9 10 8 6 4 2

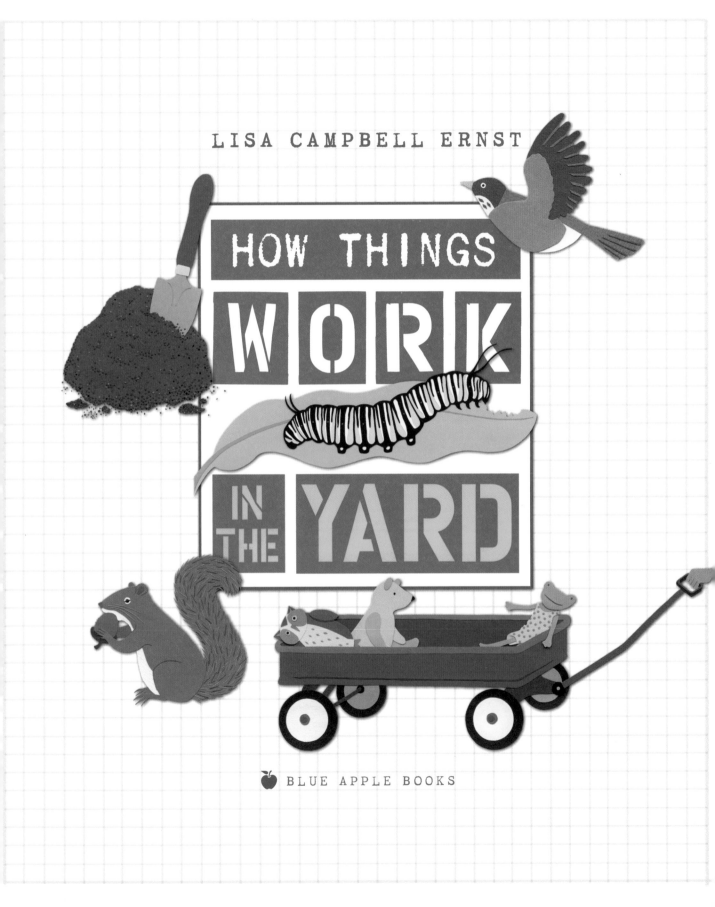

LISA CAMPBELL ERNST

HOW THINGS WORK IN THE YARD

BLUE APPLE BOOKS

A **BIRD** is an animal with feathers and wings.

This bird is a robin.

nostril

eye

ear

beak

large feathers
for flying

wing

tail

feet

small feathers
that keep the bird's body
warm and dry

Robins communicate with
each other by singing.

A robin uses the strong muscles in its chest to flap its wings.

Robins use their super eyesight to find
worms, insects, and berries to eat.

A **NEST** is a home for eggs and baby birds.

A mother robin lays eggs in a nest
she has built with help from the father
robin. Nests are shaped like bowls so that
eggs and baby birds don't fall out.

grass, twigs,
and mud

eggs

strong
branch

HOW DOES A NEST WORK?

The mother robin keeps
the eggs warm while the
father robin guards the nest.

After the eggs hatch, both parents
feed their babies until they can
fly and feed themselves.

HOW DOES A BALL WORK?

beach ball

soccer ball

A **BALL** is a round object with a surface that curves. The shape of a ball is called a sphere.

croquet ball

When a ball bounces on the ground, it squishes a little, then pushes back to its round shape.

The push against the ground sends the ball back up into the air.

baseball

snowball

golf ball

tennis ball

basketball

Balls are fun to roll, bounce, throw, and catch.

cheese ball

Never bounce, kick, or throw a cheese ball!

A ball rolls down a hill, pulled by gravity.

On flat ground, a ball rolls if pushed.

HOW DOES A
DANDELION
WORK?

A **DANDELION** is a plant with bright yellow flowers.

open seed head
Some of the seeds will become new plants.

closed seed head

flower

leaf

seed

flower bud

Roots and leaves grow from a seed.

roots underground

Wind can carry
dandelion seeds
many miles.

parachute

Dandelion flowers close at night,
then open again in the sun.

Rabbits love to eat
dandelion leaves.

You can make
a dandelion chain by
tearing a hole in a stem.
Make the opening large enough
so that you can thread another
dandelion stem through it.
Keep adding flowers
until you have a chain.

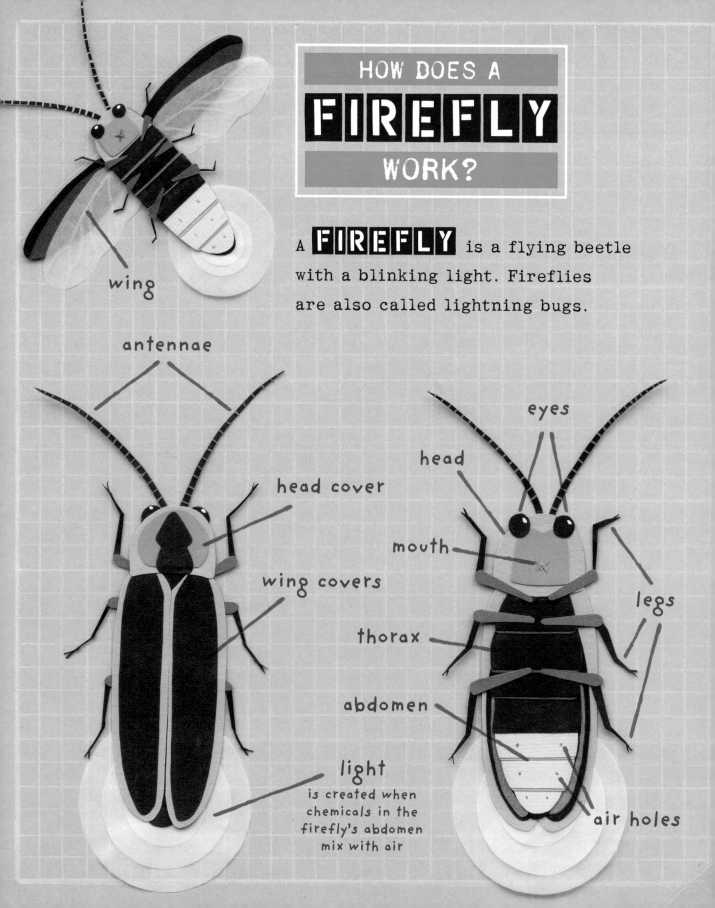

HOW DOES A
FIREFLY
WORK?

A **FIREFLY** is a flying beetle with a blinking light. Fireflies are also called lightning bugs.

wing

antennae

head cover

wing covers

light
is created when chemicals in the firefly's abdomen mix with air

eyes

head

mouth

thorax

abdomen

legs

air holes

Fireflies use their flashing
lights to find each other.
Each kind of firefly has its own
special pattern of flashing.

If you use a small flashlight
to mimic the flashing pattern you see,
a firefly might come land on your hand.

A firefly's
light is caused
by a chemical
reaction called
bioluminescence!

Try catching
fireflies and put
them in a jar with
air holes to make
a lantern for yourself.
(Remember to let the fireflies go.)

A **WHEEL** is a round disk that rolls.

HOW DOES A **WHEEL** WORK?

rim

hub

hub cap

axle

Wheels turn around a center pole called an axle. The axle stays still while the wheel spins.

18-wheelers are big trucks that get their name from their many wheels.

Wheels come in all sizes, from tiny gears in a watch to a gigantic Ferris wheel.

sideboard

A **WAGON** is a box
with four wheels.
It is used
to carry things.

handle

front bolster

HOW DOES A
WAGON
WORK?

A wagon's front
two wheels pivot
so the wagon
can turn.

Gardeners
use wagons for
moving plants,
shovels, and
flowerpots.

Small wagons have
a handle for pulling them.
Large wagons can be
pulled by horses.

HOW DOES A CATERPILLAR WORK?

A **CATERPILLAR** is an insect that will become a butterfly.

breathing holes

tentacles for feeling

prolegs

Caterpillars start their lives as tiny eggs laid by a female butterfly.

When a caterpillar hatches, its job is to eat, and eat, and eat!

Most caterpillars eat the leaves of the plant where they are born. They are like munching machines.

tentacles
for feeling

head

tiny eyes
that see only
light and dark

Caterpillars
have about
4,000 muscles
in their bodies.

true legs

jaws
that are strong
for eating

prolegs
stick tightly
to leaves and stems

After weeks of eating,
a caterpillar finds a safe spot
to rest. It becomes a chrysalis.

Caterpillars
grow at a
super-fast rate.
As they plump up,
their skin grows too tight.
The caterpillar sheds its skin
over and over again.

This caterpillar will become
a monarch butterfly.

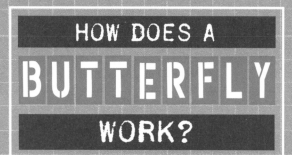

A **BUTTERFLY** is a flying insect with colorful wings.

This is a Monarch butterfly.

wings
for flying
and sensing
sound

antennae
for smelling
and balance

head

eyes

proboscis
that uncurls to sip
nectar like a straw

front legs
clean the antennae

abdomen

legs

thorax

feet that can taste

A butterfly emerges from a chrysalis. Its wings are crumpled and wet, but when they dry and straighten, the butterfly is ready to fly.

The wings of a butterfly are covered with beautiful, tiny scales that overlap.

Each kind of butterfly has its own patterns and colors.

The change from egg to butterfly is called metamorphosis!

A butterfly lays eggs on plants that will be the perfect food for the new caterpillars to eat when they hatch.

HOW DOES AN ACORN WORK?

oak leaf

cap

nut

stem

An **ACORN** is the nut, or seed, of an oak tree

When an acorn sprouts, it is a baby tree. The tree grows taller and stronger for many years before it is old enough to grow more acorns.

Squirrels love to eat acorns.
They bury them to eat in winter
when there's no other food.
Some of those acorns will sprout
to become new oak trees!

Acorns are an important food
for many animals, including pigeons,
woodpeckers, mice, and deer.

A single
oak tree can
grow more than
a thousand acorns
in one year.

A 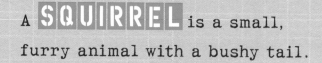**SQUIRREL** is a small, furry animal with a bushy tail.

Before a squirrel buries a nut, she licks or rubs the nut on her face to mark it with a scent. Later, she will try to find it using her sense of smell.

tail
for balance when running and jumping, an umbrella during rain, a blanket in cold weather, shade in hot weather, and a warning flag to signal other squirrels when danger is near

ears

eyes
on side of head for seeing in many directions

teeth
for cracking open nuts

claws
that are sharp for gripping trees

back legs
that are strong for leaping

HOW DOES A
SQUIRREL
WORK?

Watching squirrels jump
through trees is like
watching a circus!

Squirrels live in
dens (holes in trees),
or dreys (nests
built with
leaves).

Squirrels *love* birdseed
and are very clever
at finding it.

Squirrels chew
on tree branches
to sharpen
their teeth.

HOW DOES A
BUBBLE
WORK?

Bubbles are fun to chase and pop!

A soap **BUBBLE** is a film of soapy water filled with air.

air

Bubbles float through the air because they are so light.

inside wall

When light bounces off the inside and outside of the bubble's wall, it bends to make swirling rainbow colors.

outside wall

BUBBLE JUICE RECIPE

The holes in Swiss cheese are made by air bubbles!

Mix 1 cup of dishwashing liquid soap with 8 cups of water in a jar or bucket. Let sit overnight. Blow bubbles like crazy!

A BUBBLE WAND is a tool for blowing a bubble.

When the open end of a bubble wand is dipped into bubble juice, the liquid forms a flat film across the opening.

opening

air

handle

Gently blown air stretches the film bigger . . . and bigger . . . until the bubble is pushed out of the wand.

You can make a bubble wand from a bent wire, a paper cup, or even your fingers!

A **ROCK** is a piece of a planet's crust.

Rocks are made of small grains, called minerals, which have been squeezed or melted together. Most rocks are hard and heavy.

The many colors in rocks are made by different kinds of minerals.

Rocks with prints or pieces
of living things from long ago
are called fossils.

Some artists
carve rocks
into statues.

Strong rocks
are used to
make buildings
and walls.

You can paint
a rock to be
a silly pet!

Rocks can be as big
as a mountain,
or as tiny as
a grain of sand.

HOW DOES A SNAIL WORK?

A **SNAIL** is a little animal with a soft, slimy body protected by a hard shell.

shell

breathing hole

eyes

mouth

slimy foot
that moves like a wave for walking

A snail leaves a silver trail as it moves. The "goo" helps the snail glide.

Snails love cool, damp spaces.

Snails can walk
upside down!

tentacles
for smelling
and feeling

The curling design
of a snail's shell
is called a spiral.

The older a snail grows, the
more spirals on its shell.

When a snail is scared or hot,
it hides inside its shell.

HOW DOES DIRT WORK?

DIRT is the thin outside layer that covers the Earth's surface.

Dirt is a mixture of many things:

dead plants and animals
that have been broken into tiny pieces by bugs, worms, and other animals

rocks
that have been broken into tiny pieces by weather

air

water

Dirt is home to many creatures. Insects, worms, chipmunks, mice, and animals such as moles live in tunnels and burrows underground.

Rain mixed with dirt
makes mud: ooey, gooey,
wonderful, messy mud.

Worms tunnel
through dirt
by eating it!

Plants and dirt
help each other.
The roots of plants
keep dirt from
washing away.
The dirt protects
plants' roots.
Dirt supplies
minerals, water,
and air so plants
can grow.

HOW DOES AN ANT WORK?

ANTS are tiny insects that live and work together.

head

eye

thorax

abdomen

antennae
used for touch, smell, and taste

jaw
that is super strong

legs

hooked claw
used for climbing

queen

worker

Ants' nests are
made up of many rooms
connected by tunnels.

Ants communicate
with each other
by tapping their
antennae
together.

exoskeleton
that protects an ant's body
on the outside

Each ant has its own job.
Some look for food, some take care of baby ants,
some protect the nest, some take out the trash.
The queen lays eggs.

HOW DOES A
CLOUD
WORK?

A **CLOUD** is a collection of teeny, tiny drops of water or ice.

When the water droplets grow big and heavy, they fall to earth as rain.

In freezing weather, snow crystals form inside clouds, making snowflakes.

Clouds come in all shapes and sizes. They can look like pictures floating in the sky!

Clouds near the ground are called fog.

Puddles work best
when jumped in!

A puddle is
a bathtub
for birds.

Pebbles dropped into a
puddle make shiny ripples.

HOW DOES A
PUDDLE
WORK?

A PUDDLE
is a little pool
of water.

If the water is still and
smooth, a puddle works
like a mirror,
reflecting
the world
around it.

Leaves float
on puddles
like small
boats.

HOW DOES A HOSE WORK?

A **HOSE** is a flexible tube used to carry water.

A garden hose can help water flowers, wash a car, fill a birdbath, or just cool you off!

faucet

tube

coupling

When a hose is connected to a faucet and the handle is turned to allow water to flow, the water travels through the hose's tunnel until it shoots out the other end.

HOW DOES A **SPRINKLER** WORK?

water wheel
spins to push the
spray bar from
side to side

nozzle

connector

knob
turns to choose
spray pattern

spray jets
shoot water out

spray bar
moves back and forth

A **SPRINKLER**
is a machine that
turns hose water
into a spray of
water drops.

Water from the hose flows
into the sprinkler,
then out the little holes,
shooting high into the air.

Sprinklers
come in
different
shapes and
sizes.

BUTTERFLY

BUBBLE

PUDDLE

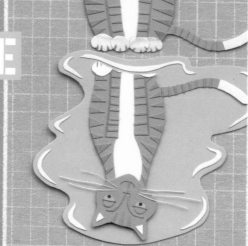

HOSE

ANT